THE STARGAZERS

An Historical Drama in Two Acts

by

Joseph Cowley

Man has weav'd out a net, and this net throwne
Upon the Heavens, and now they are his owne...

--John Donne

THE STARGAZERS

NOTE: Additional copies of *The Stargazers* may be ordered at the retail price of $11.95, plus any taxes that apply. Multiple copies, however, are discounted at 40% when ordered by drama groups or 50% when ordered by booksellers. For your convenience in ordering additional copies, there is an order form on the last page of this book.

ISBN 1-57502-259-1

Library of Congress Catalog Number: 96-96804

Printed in the USA by

M⍉RRIS
PUBLISHING

3212 E. Hwy 30
Kearney, NE 68847
800-650-7888

DEDICATION

To Timothy Ferris for the inspiration, Arthur Koestler for the title and his excellent biography of Johannes Kepler, Maryan F. Stephens and Lawrence Mattis for recognizing the play's possibilities, Inga Kimple for reading the page proofs, and the Mason Writers' Group for their kindly critiques of this and other manuscripts.

Also by Joseph Cowley:

THE CHRYSANTHEMUM GARDEN (Novel)

THE EXECUTIVE STRATEGIST: An Armchair Guide to Scientific
Decision-making (with Robert C. Weisselberg)

THE PREMISE

The planetary observations of the Danish astronomer Tycho Brahe (1546-1601) provide the data upon which Johannes Kepler (1571-1630) will later base his famous three laws accurately describing the revolutions of the planets around the sun. The play's conflict stems not only from Kepler's urgent need for Tycho's observations to prove his theories, and Tycho's equally urgent desire not to share them before he can use them (with Kepler's help) to prove his own, but also from the utterly different characters of the two men. Kepler is an advocate of the Copernican sun-centered system, Tycho of the Ptolemaic earth-centered system. Kepler's cunning and seeming weakness are pitted against Tycho's arrogance and seeming strength. At stake is the glory and fame for one of the greatest discoveries of all time: how the solar system works.

THE PLAYERS

MARIE, a serving girl, maybe 16 or 18 years old, is a true "wench." Pert and pretty, she is wise in the ways of the world and stands in awe of no man.

TYCHO DE BRAHE, 53 when the play opens, is, to quote Timothy Ferris (*Coming of Age in the Milky Way*) "an expansive, despotic giant of a man," completely bald, with a twirled handlebar mustache, "a belly of Jovian proportions, and a gleaming, metal-alloy nose (the bridge having been cut off in a youthful duel). Heroically passionate and wildly eccentric, he dresses like a prince and rules his domain like a king."

JEPP, a dwarf, is Tycho's personal servant. Wily and resourceful, he is fearful of his master, but is not so awed he is not capable of tricking or outwitting him on occasion.

JOHANNES KEPLER, 29 when the play opens, is neurotic and filled with self-loathing, but at the same time arrogant and vociferous. He comes on as a klutz, constantly tripping over himself, always apologizing, explaining, never seeming to get anywhere. Yet this is the man whom the great philosopher Immanuel Kant called "the most acute thinker ever born." Kepler is as poor as Tycho is rich.

GUNSTADT, a young man in his thirties, is a laboratory assistant to Brahe. He is ambitious, but not too bright and without discernible talent. He is the same height and build as Kepler.

i

THE SETTING

The play opens February 4, 1600, when Tycho and Johannes first meet, in Tycho's observatory at Benatky Castle, near Prague.

If you've seen *Frankenstein* or any similar "mad scientists" movie, you've seen this set before. A large room with massive stone walls and slits for windows, through which daylight may wax or wane and the stars are visible at night, its most distinctive feature is a large quadrant, stage rear, whose brass arc measures fourteen feet.

To the left of the quadrant a large, heavy wooden door leads to a corridor and the outside world. Left front is a stove used for heating and cooking, and next to it, further upstage, a cot, recently slept in, with a small rag carpet beside it.

To the right of the quadrant are sinks, shelving, and an assortment of strange-looking astronomical instruments. Further upstage there is a massive desk littered with notebooks, papers, and books. Right front a door leads to Tycho's private apartment. At stage center there is a massive wooden table with crude wooden chairs.

The room has the look of belonging to someone not overly fastidious, or too preoccupied with work to care about the immediate surroundings. The servant girl who comes in now and then to bring food or deliver a message is not often allowed to clean up or to go near the jealously-guarded data on the desk.

ACT ONE

Scene One

At Rise: *The play opens on a deserted stage. Presently we hear a thudding noise off-stage left. The door on right bursts open and JEPP, the dwarf servant, runs into the room and dives beneath the table. HE pulls the tablecloth close to hide from his master.*

TYCHO

(Roaring, off-stage) ...you bloody little bastard! *(HE enters stage right)* By God, I'll have you drawn and quartered! Where is the little beast? *(Spotting the quivering tablecloth)* Out, out, I say! *(Thudding noise goes on again. TYCHO tips the table over, sending pots and pans and notebooks and papers and beer stein crashing to the floor, to reveal the trembling JEPP)*

JEPP

Sir, sir...I beg of you...sir. It was not my fault.

TYCHO

(Raising his hand as if to strike...) You dog! You cur! You miserable little monster, sired by the Devil... *(HE suddenly becomes aware of the thudding)* Now who in the holy name of Jesus can that be? Herr Kepler? He's not to arrive until tomorrow.

JEPP

(Crawling from beneath the table) Begging your pardon, sire. Today is the fourth. He was to arrive from Graz today. The letter you read me said clearly it was to be the fourth. You...

TYCHO

(Roaring) Silence! You dare to teach me the days of the month! *(Stands there counting on his fingers. The thudding resumes off-stage. Annoyed, HE balls his fingers into a fist and waves it angrily at the dwarf)* Go, go! Are you deaf, too? Don't you hear the knocking? Must the castle fall down before you answer the door, imbecile?

JEPP

(Backing toward the door, stage left) Yes, master, it is the fourth of February, anno Domini 1600, the day Herr Kepler...

TYCHO

(Roaring) I will tell you what day it is, little monster!

JEPP

Yes, master, you will tell me what day it is, yes...

TYCHO

(*Pointing sternly*) Go! (*But as JEPP scurries toward the door, it opens and MARIE curtsies. JEPP disappears around her*)

MARIE

You called, sir?

TYCHO

(*Gruffly*) Yes...no...wait. (*Gesturing toward the overturned table*) Clean up this mess. That Jepp will be the undoing of me. I am surrounded by imbeciles.

MARIE

(*Picking up the table*) Jepp would try the patience of a saint, sir. But the learned members of your staff...

TYCHO

(*Muttering*) ...imbeciles. None of them can be trusted.

MARIE

Sir?

TYCHO

Why didn't you tell me that that scoundrel, the Junker Tengnagel, has been having an affair with my daughter Elizabeth?

MARIE

I...I...I...

TYCHO

(*Roaring*) Answer me, wench!

MARIE

I didn't know, sir...

TYCHO

I will be a laughing-stock. The father is always the last to know.

MARIE

Perhaps you are too trusting, sire.

                              TYCHO
They take advantage of my good nature.

                              MARIE
Yes, sire. I will clean up now.

                              TYCHO
Be careful. Don't break anything. I am not made of money.

                              MARIE
No, sire.

                              TYCHO
(Mumbling, wanders about the room, fiddling with the various instruments, patting the quadrant, as MARIE straightens up) They all want my riches. If it's not my money or my daughter, it's my observations they want. *(Angrily)* By God, they shall not have them! I will kill the man who... *(Crosses to the desk)*

                              MARIE
Sir, I go now. I'll take this glass and bring you fresh ones. Sir, the cook wants to know about dinner. Herr Kepler...

                              TYCHO
(Ignoring her, strikes at the papers on his desk and jumps up, knocking the chair over and shouting) Imbeciles! *(Just then the door stage left opens and JEPP enters, motioning to someone to come in, come in. KEPLER enters)*

                              MARIE
(Surprised) Herr Kepler, sir?

                              JEPP
(Grinning mischievously) Herr Kepler, sir...

                              TYCHO
(Genially) Ah, ah, my dear Herr Kepler. Come in, come in. So we meet at last! Come in, come in...

                              KEPLER
(Trying to bow and walk at the same time, almost trips, drops papers and books he has been carrying. JEPP kneels quickly and starts to gather them up) My dear Tycho...Herr Brahe...

TYCHO

(*To JEPP*) Don't touch those, you idiot! They are valuable. Both of you, out, out! (*Exit JEPP and MARIE. KEPLER makes as if to back out, too*) No, no, my dear professor. (*Bending to pick up the books and papers*) Here, let me help you. (*KEPLER suddenly bends, too. THEY bump heads. BOTH rise, looking at each other*)

KEPLER

(*Gesturing toward the door*) I, you see, the stairs... (*Sees the quadrant, looks about the room, sees the desk*) Ah...ah...

TYCHO

(*Beaming*) Welcome to Benatky Castle, Herr Kepler! And to my little laboratory, where we study the stars and the planets. And welcome to my staff, Johannes. I have looked forward to this moment...your letters...your theories have intrigued me...I...

KEPLER

Yes...I... (*Awed, steps over his books and papers on the floor, looking about, fastens again on the quadrant*) And this is your quadrant...

TYCHO

The best money could buy...the latest...

KEPLER

Yes, yes...and your desk...

TYCHO

(*Disquieted*) Yes...but your papers...

KEPLER

My papers?

TYCHO

On the floor.

KEPLER

Yes, yes, my papers! (*Turns and starts gathering them up*) I never let them out of my sight.

TYCHO

And it's no wonder. It's all there--your ingenious theories?

KEPLER

My what?

TYCHO

Your theories, Herr professor, your theories. They have intrigued me. Ingenious, yes, that's what they are...if not (*Clearing his throat*) ...as I wrote, rather a bit a priori...

KEPLER

A priori!

TYCHO

Yes. Before the facts on which they must be based. My observations...

KEPLER

Sir, I am quite capable of thinking without your observations.

TYCHO

But only my observations will prove...

KEPLER

Your observations can only prove that what I have thought out here (*Tapping his head*) and here... (*Looks about for a missing scrap of paper, spies it on the floor*) ah, yes, here... (*Holds it up*)

TYCHO

Yes, yes, a bit speculative, as I wrote. But we have the facts here, my observations of the planets. Together, we...

KEPLER

Your facts, Herr Brahe, can only buttress what the mind has thought out. Need I remind you that it is the mind that discovers the truth...not...your...facts. (*Trying to snap his fingers but not succeeding. Tries again, several times, looking at his fingers, until he finally succeeds*) Ah, yes, there. Now, where were we? You understand what I am saying?

TYCHO

(*Soothingly*) Yes, yes, well...it...a...will be very interesting to discuss this matter with you later. My servants, Jepp, did he show you to your room? At the end of the corridor? You will be sharing it with another member of...a...my staff. We dine at six.

KEPLER

Jepp? The little man?

TYCHO

Yes, Jepp, the dwarf.

KEPLER

He's a dwarf? (*Turning to look for him*)

TYCHO

(*Annoyed*) Herr professor, Herr Kepler, Herr Doctor...

KEPLER

Yes? No.

TYCHO

No, what?

KEPLER

No, they did not show me to my room.

TYCHO

I left instructions...would you like a beer? You must be weary after your long journey. Sit down, please, sit...no, no, here, at the table. (*Bellowing*) Marie! (*KEPLER, about to sit, jumps up*) No, please...sit. Marie!

MARIE

(*Enters, breathless*) You called, sir?

TYCHO

Yes...yes. Some good Danish beer for our esteemed colleague...

KEPLER

No, no, spirituous liquors only befuddle my brain.

TYCHO

And the roast we had for dinner last night. Are there perhaps a few scraps left for Herr Kepler?

KEPLER

I am too excited to eat, Herr Brahe. Your marvelous instrument...your data...they will prove my theories!

TYCHO

Yes, yes, more of that later. (*To MARIE*) Set the table for two. But, first, show Herr Kepler to his quarters...so that he might wash up. He will share Gunstadt's room.

MARIE

Gunstadt's room, sir?

TYCHO

(*Impatiently*) Yes, yes. After so long a journey...

MARIE

The room at the end of the corridor, sir, with the secret pass...

TYCHO

(*Bellowing*) Are you deaf, wench? Sir...

KEPLER

(*Jumping up*) Sir? But I've come a long way...to...to share...

TYCHO

Later, later. You will work here...for me. There will be time for sharing. I, too, look forward to hearing your wondrous theories, Herr Kepler. The planets circling the sun, five perfect Platonic solids, a model of the universe shaped like a drinking cup...the music of the spheres. Even Ptolemy (*Out of breath*) ...I am aware of your genius, sir. I have read your Cosmic Mystery.

KEPLER

Ah, my Mysterium Cosmographicum...

TYCHO

You were kind enough to send me a copy, through that scoundrel Ursus, if you remember. May he die a thousand deaths.

KEPLER

(*Embarrassed*) Yes, well, I did not mean...

TYCHO

Though I must confess, I find it difficult to believe that you are that...that very man...

KEPLER

I wrote his majesty, King Frederick, the Duke of Wuerttemberg...

TYCHO

Yes, Frederick spoke to me of your work.

KEPLER

(*Awed*) His majesty...spoke to you...of my work?

TYCHO

Yes...yes. His majesty's high opinion of you precedes you, sir. Though not everyone is in agreement with your theories. Galileo...

KEPLER

We have not corresponded for some months now.

TYCHO

Galileo?

KEPLER

No, no, the Duke. Such a kind man...such a good man. You know, then, that he had ordered a silver model of my universe...

TYCHO

Your universe!

KEPLER

To be fashioned in silver. At first it was to be but a cup, an ell in diameter, incorporating the five perfect solids, a true likeness of the world and model of the creation insofar as human reason may fathom...

TYCHO

The world to be fitted into a drinking cup forty-five inches in diameter?

KEPLER

Yes. Half a globe. The various parts to be made by different silversmiths, so that my secret would not leak out, then fitted together, the signs of the planets in precious stones the like of which has never been seen or heard of by any man...

TYCHO

I should think not!

KEPLER

(*Missing the irony*) The cup would serve seven different kinds of beverage, conducted by concealed pipes from each planetary sphere to seven taps on its rim. The sun to provide a delicious aqua vita, Mercury brandy, Venus mead...

TYCHO

(*Roaring*) Enough! Ptolemy would turn over in his grave!

KEPLER

Copernicus...

TYCHO

Silence! A pox on Copernicus! Any man who says the sun is the center of the universe when common sense and religion tell us otherwise is a dunce, sir. My observations will prove...

KEPLER

But...

TYCHO

Silence! I will not have that fool's name mentioned in my presence. Not if we are to get on with our work. (*An awkward silence. More gently, seeing the distress on Kepler's face*) Go on, Herr Kepler. I did not mean...then what happened?

KEPLER

His majesty did not want the cosmic mystery in the shape of a drinking cup. He wanted a celestial globe. I made a paper model of it, but it would not work. In its stead I proposed a mobile planetarium...to reproduce the motions of the heavens within an error of one degree for the next six or ten thousand years. But I was much too ambitious. It would have cost a fortune...

TYCHO

(*Ironic again*) Undoubtedly.

KEPLER

I wrote to Maestlin that, if the Duke agreed, it would be best to break up the whole junk and refund the silver to him. The Duke was reluctant to abandon our project, but...

TYCHO

Yes, yes, all that can wait until later. We will have a chance to talk over the supper table. Let Marie show you to your quarters. You will want to wash up, and perhaps rest before our work begins. The night is young, Herr Kepler, and the stars wait.

KEPLER

Ah, yes, the stars!

MARIE

This way, Herr Kepler...

KEPLER

I'd rather...

TYCHO

Later, Herr Kepler.

KEPLER

But you are too kind, sir. Your obedient servant... (*Bowing, follows* MARIE *out*)

TYCHO

(*Waits impatiently for them to exit, then pounces with glee on two sheets of paper on the floor that* KEPLER *has overlooked*) Aha! The theory, the theory...that shall...make my observations... (*Waves the papers in the air*) Ptolemy, Ptolemy! With the help of this worm...this...this (*Scornfully*) theorist, I, Tycho de Brahe, shall build you an edifice you will be proud of! We two are the greatest astronomers who have ever... (*Voice trails off as he reads, at first mumbling to himself, then aloud. Does not see* JEPP *sneak into the room and hide beneath the table*) "Who has ever dared before to think, and much less to try to expose and explain a priori and, so to speak, out of the hidden knowledge of the Creator, the number, order, magnitude, and motion of the spheres? But Kepler has undertaken and successfully done just this..." Bah! No one can...

JEPP

(*Peeks from beneath the table, holding the tablecloth about his neck, and wags his head at the audience. Sotto voce*) But Kepler has...

TYCHO

(*Looks about, not sure he hasn't heard something. Continues to read, aloud*) "Henceforth shall be freed from the necessity of exploring the dimensions of the spheres a posteriori, that is by the method of observations (many of which are inexact and not to say doubtful)..." Pah! Only a letter from that fool Maestlin, Kepler's old professor. A theory without the facts is not worth the dunce-head who thinks it up. No one will... (*Drops the page on the floor to read the next sheet*)

JEPP
(*Same as before*) But Kepler has...

TYCHO
(*Again momentarily distracted before continuing*) But what's this, a letter from the dunce-head himself? (*Holding it up to the light, reads aloud*) "Let all keep silence and hark to Tycho, who has devoted thirty-five years to his observations..." Yes, yes, he knows how great their value. (*Reading on, mumbling at first, then aloud*) "For Tycho alone do I wait; he shall explain to me the order and arrangement of the orbits..."

JEPP
(*As before*) Yes, yes, Tycho shall...

TYCHO
(*Angrily*) Will he now? So Kepler can take credit for my work! (*Reading on*) "Then I hope I shall one day, if God keeps me alive, erect a wonderful edifice." (*Raising his fists aloft and crying loudly*) If God keeps you alive, Herr Kepler...if God keeps you alive! Damned villain...varlet...knave...

JEPP
(*Sliding from beneath the table*) You called for me, Master?

(*End of Scene One*)

Scene Two

At Rise: *Later that evening, scene as before. Remains of a*
                    meal strew the table. Sounds of revelry off-stage.
                    Door to Tycho's apartment opens. JEPP *peers into*
                    the room, then crosses to the table and feasts
                    hurriedly on the scraps. Large door in rear creaks
                    open and JEPP *dives beneath the table.* GUNSTADT
                    enters, crosses to the desk, and leafs through the
                    papers. JEPP *pokes his head from beneath the table.*

JEPP

(*Loudly*) Hah!

GUNSTADT

(*Startled*) Ah! (*Turns, backing against the desk*)

JEPP

(*Wagging a finger at him*) Nosy, nosy! (*Crawls from beneath the table*) Master
would not like.

GUNSTADT

(*Not very convincingly*) I...I was looking for the observations I made last
night. I left them here...on the desk. I made mistakes.

JEPP

A likely story. You came to steal the master's secrets.

GUNSTADT

Not true!

JEPP

So much the worse for you, then. You know our master's passion for
precision. (*Imitating Tycho*) Precision, precision, precision! Imbecile! (*In his
own voice*) He'll have you drawn and quartered.

GUNSTADT

But...

JEPP

Now, if you had only come to steal a few tidbits...

GUNSTADT

You would not tell!

JEPP

You would merely be shot.

GUNSTADT

Please...I beg of you...

JEPP

Oh, I assure you...

GUNSTADT

Thank God!

JEPP

I can be bribed.

GUNSTADT

Bribed?

JEPP

Bought.

GUNSTADT

But I have nothing!

JEPP

The master pays you nothing?

GUNSTADT

Not a pfennig. It is a privilege and honor to work for such a great man. He treats me well.

JEPP

Yes, yes, we live like kings here--feasting...

GUNSTADT

Yes.

JEPP

And carrying on with his maid-servant.

GUNSTADT

Marie? You!

JEPP

No, you, Herr Gunstadt. Don't think I haven't been aware. Nothing escapes
my notice. And when the master hears...

GUNSTADT

You wouldn't tell!

JEPP

I am his eyes and ears, Herr Gunstadt. He trusts me to keep him informed.

GUNSTADT

Can't we work something out? I will do anything.

JEPP

Like what?

GUNSTADT

Like...I don't know. I have nothing.

JEPP

You have Marie.

GUNSTADT

Marie?

JEPP

And Marie has the keys to the wine cellar.

GUNSTADT

Wine cellar?

JEPP

Come, come, Herr Gunstadt. You lack imagination.

GUNSTADT

You mean...

JEPP

(*Impatiently*) Yes, yes. A bottle of wine now and then and my lips are sealed.
You and Marie...

GUNSTADT

That's all? Then it's settled?

JEPP

It's settled. Let's not speak of it again.

GUNSTADT

Oh, my dear Jepp, you are most magnanimous. I will be forever in your debt!

JEPP

(*Slyly*) Yes, you will. But as for this other thing...

GUNSTADT

Other thing? I don't understand.

JEPP

This matter of stealing the master's data.

GUNSTADT

But I never...would never! I am too loyal...I owe too much...

JEPP

So much the worse for you, then. Do you know what the master's observations are worth?

GUNSTADT

Yes...no...

JEPP

They are worth a king's ransom. Not just those you will find in the desk there, though they would fetch enough. But I know where the master keeps the many volumes in which...

GUNSTADT

You wouldn't dare!

JEPP

No, not I. But you. Together we might...

GUNSTADT

But only a prince would have the wealth to reward, and protect, those who brought him such gifts.

JEPP

Exactly.

GUNSTADT

And even to a prince they would be worthless without...

JEPP

Yes?

GUNSTADT

A genius to understand and make sense of them.

JEPP

(*Smiling*) You are brighter than I gave you credit for, Herr Gunstadt.

GUNSTADT

But I...I am not that genius.

JEPP

Obviously not!

GUNSTADT

Then?

JEPP

Don't you see?

GUNSTADT

I'm afraid I don't.

JEPP

We now have them both...here...in this castle.

GUNSTADT

I don't understand. (*Sound of laughing and loud talk in the corridor. A light dawns*) You don't mean...

JEPP

Exactly!

(*End of Scene Two*)

Scene Three

At Rise: *Same scene as before. Laughing and talking, TYCHO and KEPLER enter rear.*

GUNSTADT

Herr Kepler?

JEPP

(Smiling) Yes, Herr Kepler. *(HE puts his finger to his lips)*

KEPLER

(Surprised at hearing his name) Yes?

TYCHO

Ah, yes, Herr Kepler. You have met my son Joergen, who is in charge of the laboratory, and Herr Longomontanus, my senior assistant. Now meet Herr Gunstadt, another of my laboratory assistants. He will be sharing the room with you...

GUNSTADT

(Humbly) If I can be of any service to you, Herr Kepler. Your fame precedes you...

TYCHO

(Annoyed) Yes, yes, now leave us. Herr Kepler and I have matters to discuss...

JEPP

(Mocking) Matters of the gravest discourse.

TYCHO

(Scowling) Out, out, both of you...before I lose my temper. *(As JEPP and GUNSTADT leave, HE turns expansively to Kepler)* Some of my largest instruments have not yet arrived from Uraniburg, my laboratory at Hven. We have been here only six months, but already you can see...

KEPLER

Yes, yes, most impressive, Herr Brahe.

TYCHO

As my poems inscribed over the entrance to the castle make clear, I intend
here to build another Uraniburg. I had there in Denmark the greatest
astronomical laboratory in the world. King Christian will be sorry indeed that
he lost me. But here, near Prague...

KEPLER

Such a magnificent castle! And a separate gate for the Emperor?

TYCHO

Yes. I am reserving an adjoining building for his visits.

KEPLER

I shall be most flattered.

TYCHO

You are too easily awed, Herr Kepler. It is they who must, and quite fittingly
do, stand in awe of us...stargazers. (*Patting the quadrant*) With instruments
like this, we explore the stars, unlock the secrets of the universe...

KEPLER

(*Timidly*) I have never used a quadrant before.

TYCHO

(*Astounded*) Never used a quadrant! But how...

KEPLER

I used a piece of wood from a workshop, suspended from the ceiling with a
length of rope, for my sightings.

TYCHO

(*Roaring with laughter*) A what?!

KEPLER

You may well laugh, but my crude staff was sufficiently precise to show the
variation of a half a degree in the positions of the polar star when sighted from
extreme points of the earth's path, if, as one might expect...

TYCHO

(*Smiling sarcastically*) The earth's path?

KEPLER

The earth moves, Herr Brahe. Around the sun. Copernicus...

TYCHO

Pah! You are a bigger fool than I thought, Herr Kepler, to give credence to
the ravings of that madman. Has your religious upbringing taught you nothing?
The earth is at the center of the universe. Man, made in God's image, inhabits
the earth, as is right and proper. Your theories will not change that.

KEPLER

No, but your observations will. Even my crude observations of the polar star
showed... (*HE hesitates*)

TYCHO

(*Impatient*) Showed what?

KEPLER

Nothing

TYCHO

Nothing?

KEPLER

No stellar parallax. No apparent shift in the apparent position of the fixed
stars.

TYCHO

I am disappointed in you, Johannes. If you had read my book...

KEPLER

De Nova Stella.

TYCHO

Yes. On the nova of 1572. My observations proved it was a new star because
it did not move.

KEPLER

And because the stars do not move, it means...

TYCHO

(*Contemptuously*) The earth stands still, Herr Kepler.

KEPLER

(*Slyly*) Or the universe is immeasurably larger than we think it is, Herr Brahe.
At least five hundred times larger.

TYCHO

You are mad! Five hundred times larger? Is man, then, a mere flea in God's eyes?

KEPLER

An enlarged universe does not diminish man's moral stature, Herr Brahe. Otherwise the crocodile or the elephant would be nearer to God's heart than man, because they are larger.

TYCHO

Your thinking is Jesuitical, Herr Kepler, and just as false.

KEPLER

You cling to Ptolemy.

TYCHO

I have my own "Tychonic" theory.

KEPLER

And that theory is?

TYCHO

That the planets revolve about the sun while the sun revolves around the earth.

KEPLER

And the earth stands still?

TYCHO

How could it be otherwise? If the earth moved, we would be flung off into the ether, sir. Besides, what need is there for the earth to move? God made it the center of the universe so that it might be the proper home for man and bade the sphere of the stars wheel nightly overhead in their diurnal journey around it.

KEPLER

That is Ursus the Bear's theory.

TYCHO

It is my theory. Ursus stole it from me!

KEPLER

Stole it from you? But how? When?

TYCHO

When he visited me some years ago with his benefactor, Sir Lange.

KEPLER

But what proof...?

TYCHO

I trust no one, you understand. Because I suspected him of snooping among my papers, I took the precaution of having Andreas, one of my pupils, share his room. When Ursus was asleep, Andreas went through his breeches and found a handful of papers in one of his pockets.

KEPLER

Your papers?

TYCHO

Yes. Andreas would have gone through the other pocket but stopped for fear of waking the Bear.

KEPLER

What did Ursus say when you confronted him?

TYCHO

He behaved like a maniac. I would have shot him on the spot were it not for the presence of his benefactor. Instead, I restored those papers that did not concern me and sent him off.

KEPLER

And he had your theory in his other pocket?

TYCHO

Draw your own conclusions. Four years later he published the system of the universe as his own in his Fundaments of Astronomy. Except for minor details, it was the one I had worked out.

KEPLER

Yes, yes, I seem to remember...

TYCHO

Seem to remember! Why, you scoundrel, you wrote him a letter of praise that was published in the book along with the theory!

KEPLER

I...I did not mean the letter to see the light of day.

TYCHO

But you wrote it!

KEPLER

It was years before Ursus published his book. I was a nonentity then, searching for a famous man who would praise my new discovery of how the five perfect solids fit the orbits of the planets. If, in the selfish desire to flatter him, I blurted out words which exceeded my opinion of him, this is to be explained by the impulsiveness of youth.

TYCHO

Such an elaborate apology, Herr Kepler! There's no need. After all, it's water over the dam.

KEPLER

But Ursus...

TYCHO

Him I can't forgive! He disemboweled me in his book. My only regret is that I didn't kill the bastard when I had the chance.

KEPLER

But his theory is useless without your observations to prove...

TYCHO

You and I are in utter agreement, Herr Kepler! Any jackass can make up a theory. But today, with our modern instruments of measurement, all theories must fit the facts, the precise data...

KEPLER

And no data is more precise, Herr Brahe, than those resulting from your many years of continuous observations.

TYCHO

My observations are what everyone wants. (Slyly) Even you, Herr Kepler.

KEPLER

I don't deny...though no one has seen...you have the data?

TYCHO

Yes, yes, they are all here (*Turning toward the desk*), here in...

KEPLER

The desk?

TYCHO

(*HE stops and wags his finger at Kepler*) You are much cleverer by far, Herr Kepler. Some of the data I keep in the desk. The rest I keep elsewhere...hidden...so that it will be safe from...

KEPLER

From?

TYCHO

(*Glowering at him*) Scoundrels!

KEPLER

(*Taken aback*) Surely you don't think...

TYCHO

I haven't spent a lifetime of sleepless nights in damp, cold hell-holes like this one, my hands numb, my teeth chattering, my bones aching, to be cheated out of the glory that is mine!

KEPLER

But everyone knows of your work, Herr Brahe, of the precision and scope of your measurements of the heavens, and of your marvelous instruments. No one can rob you of the glory.

TYCHO

I would kill the man who tries!

KEPLER

Then why not protect yourself by publishing, Herr Brahe? Hasn't the world waited long enough?

TYCHO

My observations are not complete. Besides, data, like jewels, need a setting, a conceptual framework to show off their beauty. The Tychonic theory...

KEPLER

Your theory that the sun orbits the earth while the planets orbit the sun?

TYCHO

Yes. The facts will prove...

KEPLER

If that's what your observations prove, Herr Brahe, then I bow to your superior genius. But I thought...

TYCHO

Yes?

KEPLER

That you invited me here because...because...my own theories...

TYCHO

You flatter yourself, Herr Kepler. I invited you here because I needed an assistant, and you come highly recommended. Some of my assistants at Uraniburg, though they promised to come with me, have declined now to leave their native Denmark.

KEPLER

Yes, yes. And I am grateful, Herr Brahe. But I left Graz before your letter of invitation arrived. It only caught up with me on the road. You see, you were my only hope.

TYCHO

(*Puzzled*) For your theories?

KEPLER

For my person. For my poor wife and children. I have been exiled from Germany...because I am a Lutheran and would not recant. Not even the university would permit me to keep my post.

TYCHO

Pah! You are not the first, and you will not be the last, genius to be driven from that overweening poppycock of a nation. They have no tolerance for the truth if it disagrees with their set ideas.

KEPLER

Still, though they deprive me of a livelihood, I miss...

TYCHO

But you will make a new home here. Here you are among friends. Here you will be free to theorize to your heart's content, and to gaze at the stars...

KEPLER

Ah, the stars. Yes, they are eternal. If only we could fathom...

TYCHO

You are filled with theories, Herr Kepler. But here we deal with the facts, you understand?

KEPLER

But of course, Herr Brahe. I know that only precise data on mean distances and eccentricities can determine whether a stellar parallax exists or not, and thus whether...

TYCHO

Whether Copernicus or Ptolemy is right...and thus whether Johannes Kepler or Tycho de Brahe is right.

KEPLER

Yes. The answer is in the stars. Only precise observations...

TYCHO

But will you have the patience to sit here night after night in this gloomy dungeon--for that is what it will become to you--your eyes glued to the heavens while the cold seeps into your bones and your body grows weary for sleep?

KEPLER

You have but to try me, Herr Brahe. Name me a task.

TYCHO

Tomorrow. You must be weary after your long journey. I'm sure Marie has made your bed and put a warming pan among the sheets.

KEPLER

I am too excited to sleep. Let us but make a beginning, Herr Brahe. We are on the brink of discovering the secrets of the universe, the mathematical laws that govern the movements of the planets...the harmony of the spheres! They are there...somewhere in your data. I am certain of it. Let us find them together, Herr Brahe! Trust me...share with me...

TYCHO

(*Laughing*) How you do get carried away, Herr Kepler! (*Turning away*) But, then, you are young. When one is young it is easy to believe...any schemes...no matter how wild.

KEPLER

You are the only man in all the world who possesses the exact data needed to prove whether my theories are wild or not, Herr Brahe. Share your observations with me!

TYCHO

I have been told that you are a genius. (*Shrugging*) Perhaps they are right. We shall see. But we must work together, you understand. You will take orders from me.

KEPLER

Yes, yes! I apprentice myself to you. But let us make a beginning.

TYCHO

Tomorrow. (*Looks at the quadrant and up at the night sky, stars showing through the high windows, and gestures*) My day is only beginning. Go to bed. We will talk about it tomorrow.

KEPLER

Give me a task to ponder while I sleep.

TYCHO

A task?

KEPLER

Yes.

TYCHO

What kind of task?

KEPLER

Anything.

TYCHO

(*Slyly*) Anything?

KEPLER

Yes. A task I can dream upon.

TYCHO

Can you be persuaded to apply your theory of the five perfect solids to my own theory of the universe?

KEPLER

(*Making a face*) Anything but that.

TYCHO

So, already we disagree! Well...

KEPLER

Perhaps...

TYCHO

Quiet! I am thinking. (*After a moment*) Aha! I have it! You are familiar with that detested book of Ursus we spoke of? The one in which he so contemptuously abused me?

KEPLER

Yes.

TYCHO

Then your first task shall be to write a refutation, which we shall publish to the world...

KEPLER

But, sir, the stars...

TYCHO

The stars?

KEPLER

I would find such a task onerous.

TYCHO

(*Shouting*) The book is an abomination!

KEPLER

But it has been more than ten years...and Ursus is dead.

TYCHO

I did not mean to keep your from your stargazing. If you will write this refutation...in your spare time, of course, then...then I will give you a task worthy of your genius.

KEPLER

You will be my benefactor, sir.

TYCHO

Yes, well, I meant to put you in charge of the next planet to be taken up for systematic observation...but, since Longomontanus seems to be getting nowhere with Mars...

KEPLER

Mars! That is more than I ever hoped...

TYCHO

Then you will do this trifle for me?

KEPLER

You honor me, sir.

TYCHO

I must warn you. It is the most difficult of all the planets. Its eccentricities have baffled the greatest...

KEPLER

Yes, yes. I will have it solved within the week.

TYCHO

Within the week!

KEPLER

Yes. I would bet my life on it.

TYCHO

That you will have determined the orbit of Mars within a week?

KEPLER

Eight days at the most.

TYCHO

And would you wager on that?

KEPLER

Yes.

TYCHO

Would you wager your theories against my observations?

KEPLER

I don't understand, sir.

TYCHO

If I lose, I put my observations at your disposal. I give you free rein to study them at will, nothing withheld.

KEPLER

And if *I* lose, which is not likely?

TYCHO

If you lose, sir, I will request that you give your best thought to applying your theory of the five perfect solids to my own theory of the universe--until I give you permission to desist.

KEPLER

You drive a hard bargain. But determining the orbit of Mars would be a great challenge.

TYCHO

Is it a wager then?

KEPLER

It is, sir.

TYCHO

Eight days to determine the true orbit of Mars?

KEPLER

Here is my hand on it.

TYCHO

(*Shaking his hand*) Good! Now get you to bed. Your trial will begin tomorrow. You will need a clear head.

KEPLER

You have given me something to dream on, Herr Brahe. I shall use my sleep to ponder this problem. It is a happy challenge indeed!

TYCHO

Dream well, Herr Kepler.

KEPLER

(*Bowing his way out*) Your obedient servant, sir. (*HE exits*)

TYCHO

(*Exultant*) The fool! The utter fool! It will take years, not days, to solve that problem, and more genius than he or any man has to solve it in even that time! (*Raising his fists and eyes toward the heavens*) Ptolemy, we have won, you and I! The great Kepler is about to join our team!

(*End of Scene Three*)

Scene Four

At Rise: Scene same as before, the hour before dawn. It is very dark.
Starlight and light from beneath the great door illuminate the
stage. TYCHO, *covered by a blanket, is asleep on the cot. The*
door opens, sending light across the stage. A SHADOWY
FIGURE *enters, crosses to the desk, and rifles through the*
papers. Wakened, TYCHO *sits up in the dark.*

TYCHO

(Shouting) Ho, damned villain! Varlet! Knave! *(Rising)* Steal my treasure, will
you! *(Loud explosion and blinding flash. The* SHADOWY FIGURE *groans and
slumps to the floor. For a few seconds there is only silence, then we hear the
sound of voices and running footsteps in the corridor.* JEPP *bursts into the room
carrying a lantern.* TYCHO *stands by the cot, a gun in his hand)*

JEPP

Master, master, I thought they had killed you! Have they killed you? I do not
see the blood.

TYCHO

(Too stunned to speak) Ah-ah-ah...

MARIE

*(Entering, sees Tycho's mute state and shakes her head disapprovingly. Crosses
to the table and lights the candles. As stage lights up, sees the body on the
floor and backs away, speechless with fright)* Ah...ah...

JEPP

(Turning) What...who...is it?

MARIE

I do not know. He is dead.

JEPP

But who?

TYCHO

K-K-Kepler. The scoundrel!

JEPP and MARIE (*Together*)

Kepler!

TYCHO

He tried to rob me. I knew he would try.

MARIE

But, sir...

TYCHO

He deserved to die.

JEPP

A genius?

TYCHO

A thief!

JEPP

But, sir...you said he was the only one in the whole of Europe who could make sense out of your data. You said...

TYCHO

Pah! He was nothing but... (*Suddenly aware*) Oh, my God, what have I done! (*Throws the gun on the cot*) I've killed him! (*Stumbles to the front of the stage*) My genius! (*Falls to his knees and raises his hands in supplication*) Forgive me, God. You sent Kepler to me that I might use his brain to...to...forgive me, forgive me...Herr Kepler, forgive me! (*Weeps*) Together, we...the secrets of the universe. A genius...yes, a genius... O Lord...forgive me...what have I done! (*Weeping, does not hear the FIGURE ON THE FLOOR groan. JEPP and MARIE hear the groans and look at each other with puzzled expressions. While TYCHO continues his lamentations, JEPP cautiously approaches the body and turns it over with his foot*)

JEPP

Gunstadt!

MARIE

Gunstadt?

TYCHO

Gunstadt!

JEPP

Yes, Gunstadt.

TYCHO

Dead?

MARIE

Gunstadt, dead!

JEPP

(*Bending over the body*) No, not dead.

MARIE

Gunny! (*Rushes to Gunstadt and kneels over him, weeping*) Oh, Gunny, Gunny, my sweet Gunny. Speak to me!

TYCHO

(*Looking at audience*) Gunny?

JEPP

Gunstadt, sir.

TYCHO

(*Irritated, HE rises and brushes himself off*) I know who Gunstadt is. If he isn't dead, I shall kill him.

JEPP

He isn't dead, sire. There is no blood. Shall I reload your gun?

GUNSTADT

(*Groaning, HE sits up*) Oh, oh...

TYCHO

(*Growling*) Scoundrel. You came to steal...

MARIE

(*Protectively*) Oh, no, sir. Herr Gunstadt...

GUNSTADT

(*Slowly rising, feels himself all over*) Oh, no, sir. Some of my figures are in error. I came to correct...Jepp knows...

TYCHO

Errors! You made errors?

JEPP

Yes, errors, sire. He came to correct...

TYCHO

(*Roaring*) And you are not dead! (*Dives for the gun on the cot and starts to reload it with trembling hands*)

MARIE

(*Jumping in front of Gunstadt*) Oh, no, sire!

JEPP

(*To Gunstadt*) See what I told you, fool! It is better to be a thief. Now you will surely die.

MARIE

(*Throwing herself at Tycho's feet*) Oh, sir, I beg of you...

TYCHO

(*To Gunstadt, incredulously*) And have you also been dipping into my servant's love box, sir? You are a greater knave than I gave you credit for!

JEPP

(*Counting on his fingers*) One, a thief. Two, a fool. Three, a knave. Oh, this jackass must surely die.

GUNSTADT

Oh, sire, I am your humble servant, your loyal, humble servant...

MARIE

(*Clutching Tycho's arm*) Oh, sir, sir, I beg of you...

TYCHO

Unhand me, wench. This dog must die!

KEPLER

(*Entering as* THEY *struggle, unaware of anything untoward*) Mars is in the ascendant. It is in conjunction with the sun and will rise but an hour or two before dawn. Excuse me, Herr Brahe, I must begin my work. The planet is as bright as it will ever be this night. (*Swings the quadrant into position for sighting.* TYCHO, JEPP, *and* GUNSTADT *look at one another*)

TYCHO

Out, out, fools!

MARIE and GUNSTADT (*Together*)

But, sir...

TYCHO

(*Angrily*) Can't you see Herr Kepler has work to do?

JEPP

But, sir, you were going to kill Herr Gunstadt.

TYCHO

Later, later. Go, go. Herr Gunstadt...

KEPLER

(*Turning*) Ah, yes, Herr Gunstadt. Does he take dictation? Can he make notes of my observations as I speak them?

GUNSTADT

(*Stepping forward, eagerly*) Oh, yes, sir. That is what I do best.

JEPP

(*Slyly, glancing at Marie*) Only one of the things you do best.

TYCHO

(*Scowling*) Out, out! Let us leave Herr Kepler to his work. Marie, fetch Herr Kepler some breakfast. Some beer, and maybe some of the roast beef left over from last night. And some cheese. Let him taste our good Danish cheese. And a dried apple, Herr Kepler?

KEPLER

What?

TYCHO

A dried apple?

KEPLER

A dried apple?

TYCHO

For your breakfast.

KEPLER

Dried apple. Yes. And eggs. Boiled eggs. Yes. And tea. You have herbal tea? It settles my nerves and is good for the scrofula and other diseases. My health is not the best.

MARIE

But Herr Gunstadt, sir...

TYCHO

I will deal with him later. Out, out, all of you.

MARIE

Oh, sir...

TYCHO

(*To Gunstadt, who starts out*) Not you, idiot! Be grateful Herr Kepler needs your help. But if you make any more mistakes...

GUNSTADT

Oh, no, sire. I don't know how I could have...

TYCHO

(*Pushing the others out the door*) Imbecile!

KEPLER

Sir?

TYCHO

No, no, not you, Herr Kepler. Herr Gunstadt...

KEPLER

Ah, yes, Herr Gunstadt. Do you have paper and pen?

GUNSTADT

Yes, Herr Kepler. Right here on the desk.

KEPLER

(*Sighting along the quadrant*) Yes, yes, I can see it quite clearly. I have it now. Do you have the time?

GUNSTADT

Yes, Herr Kepler. It is... (*Studying a timepiece along the far wall that Tycho has devised*) It is...

KEPLER

Don't tell me. Write it down, write it down. Be precise. Here is the first reading. Exactly, now, as I pronounce it.

GUNSTADT

Yes, sir, exactly...

TYCHO

(*Meaningfully*) Exactly. (*Takes one last look at Gunstadt and sneers before exiting*) Gunny!

(*End of Scene Four*)

Scene Five

At Rise: *Scene same as before, a few hours later, daylight.*
                    KEPLER and GUNSTADT, spent, sit at table picking at
                    the enormous amount of food TYCHO has sent up.

KEPLER

But he meant you no harm.

GUNSTADT

No harm? He meant to kill me!

KEPLER

You can't blame the man for feeling as he does about his data. He possesses
the best observations in all the world. A life-time of precise, continuous data...

GUNSTADT

But he is a mean-spirited man, a tyrant. He is dangerous.

KEPLER

You are upset, Herr Gunstadt. Herr Brahe is a great astronomer. There is no
one like him. He only lacks the architect who would put all this data to use
according to his own design.

GUNSTADT

I warn you for your own good, Herr Kepler. He is rich...

KEPLER

Superlatively rich. But he knows not how to make proper use of his wealth,
as is the case with most rich people. We must find some way to wrest it from
him so that it can be put to good use.

GUNSTADT

Steal?!

KEPLER

No, no, no. We must be more crafty than that. Persuade.

GUNSTADT

But he is used to having his own way.

KEPLER

Not in the realm of ideas. (*Unobserved, JEPP sneaks into the room from Tycho's apartment and stands listening*) We will have to use our wits to get around the man's suspicious nature...his mania. If I could but find a way to study his observations...

JEPP

Planning another theft, Herr Gunstadt?

GUNSTADT

(*Startled*) I did not hear you come in.

JEPP

That is the story of your life.

GUNSTADT

Where is the master?

JEPP

(*Off-handedly*) Asleep. He will sleep till noon, as is usual. I left him snoring loudly. (*Making himself comfortable*) But do go on, Herr Kepler. I find your disclosure fascinating.

GUNSTADT

We...we were discussing nothing.

JEPP

Nothing?

GUNSTADT

Only matters of a technical nature. They would not interest you.

JEPP

How can you be so sure, Herr Gunstadt? It seems to me I distinctly heard Herr Kepler say he would like to find a way to study Herr Brahe's observations.

KEPLER

It was but the expression of an idle wish. I'm sure Herr Brahe...

JEPP

Are you trying to cut me out of my own plan, Herr Gunstadt? I thought we had come to an accommodation...

GUNSTADT

It was nothing...nothing.

JEPP

Would you have me go to the master with this news I overheard?

GUNSTADT

I assure you. Herr Kepler was just saying...

JEPP

That great minds run in the same groove, Herr Gunstadt?

GUNSTADT

Yes...no! I swear...our plan...

KEPLER

What plan?

GUNSTADT

No plan, Herr Kepler. It is nothing. Jepp...

JEPP

I have but to say the word...

GUNSTADT

I have said nothing!

JEPP

I am no fool, Herr Gunstadt, though I play the fool...

GUNSTADT

He knows nothing, I assure you. I have not broached the subject.

KEPLER

What subject?

JEPP

We have a little scheme, Herr Kepler, that will permit you to study Herr
Brahe's observations...as was your expressed desire.

KEPLER

Enough, gentlemen! There is no need for plans and scheming. Herr Brahe
himself has agreed to share his observations with me within the week...as soon

as I determine the orbit of Mars.

GUNSTADT

The orbit of Mars!

KEPLER

Yes. We have a wager.

GUNSTADT

That will take years!

KEPLER

Days, Herr Gunstadt, days. With your help.

GUNSTADT

But...

JEPP

We can be patient, Herr Gunstadt. Herr Kepler needs time...

KEPLER

Yes, yes...just a week...

JEPP

Where others have failed, Herr Kepler may succeed...(*Aside*) in learning of our master's nasty disposition. (*To Kepler*) A week, you say?

KEPLER

Eight days, to be precise. And in my spare time I shall write a refutation of the Bear's Fundaments of Astronomy.

GUNSTADT

In your spare time!

JEPP

Patience, Herr Gunstadt, patience. (*To Kepler*) And if you fail?

KEPLER

Then my thinking, my theories, will be at Herr Brahe's disposal.

GUNSTADT

The sly devil! No one can beat him at this game he plays.

KEPLER

Game?

GUNSTADT

To get and keep all he has. He is ruthless.

JEPP

Now, now, Herr Gunstadt, you slander our master.

GUNSTADT

What does it matter? He will surely let me go. When he wakes and remembers...

JEPP

How hasty he was in firing his gun at you? It was foolish of him. He might have killed Herr Kepler here...

KEPLER

What? Why would he kill...

JEPP

He would not hesitate to kill you, Herr Kepler, if he thought you were about to steal his secrets.

GUNSTADT

You saw what he did last night...shooting at me in the dark. He is a most dangerous opponent.

JEPP

You see his nose. He lost the bridge in a duel when he was young. The other man died.

KEPLER

I have no need to steal his observations. He will willingly share them a week from now, when I have determined the orbit of Mars.

GUNSTADT

No one has solved the mystery of the orbit of Mars. He will suck your brain dry, Herr Kepler, and use your ideas to his own glory.

KEPLER

We shall see who will win out.

JEPP

We have a plan, Herr Kepler...

KEPLER

I have no need for a plan.

JEPP

So you say now. But a week from now?

GUNSTADT

He's a sly one, Herr Kepler. He plays his cards close to his vest.

JEPP

Herr Brahe may call you his dear friend and smile at you, but it is all to cozen you.

GUNSTADT

He will never share any practical knowledge with you.

JEPP

He will dangle data in front of you like bait, just enough to keep you working for him until he has sucked you clean.

GUNSTADT

Today it will be something about the apogee of one planet, tomorrow something about the nodes of another.

JEPP

Scraps of information.

GUNSTADT

Tossed to you as he tosses scraps of food to Jepp here.

JEPP

For which I play the fool.

KEPLER

And your plan?

JEPP

Herr Brahe's observations will bring a king's ransom from...from...the right king.

KEPLER
For whom? You? Gunstadt?

JEPP
And you, Herr Kepler.

KEPLER
Me?!

GUNSTADT
The observations will be yours...

JEPP
(*Aside*) And you will be ours.

GUNSTADT
To use to prove your theories.

KEPLER
Pah! You malign the man. Besides, his observations...

GUNSTADT
Which you will never see.

JEPP
So long as he is alive.

KEPLER
(*Tired of their scheming*) Then I await his death.

JEPP
(*Gleefully*) Now we are getting somewhere.

GUNSTADT
But after his death there will be his wife and son to contend with. They know the value of his observations.

KEPLER
And less what to do with them than Herr Brahe himself. There is only myself...

JEPP
And the Junker Tengnagel.

GUNSTADT

Tengnagel?!

JEPP

To contend with. He has gotten Brahe's daughter Elisabeth with child.

GUNSTADT

You don't say!

JEPP

I do say.

GUNSTADT

I didn't even know he was pumping her.

JEPP

You still think such things can be kept secret?

KEPLER

Enough, gentlemen! You indulge now in idle gossip, and I have work to do. The sun has paled Mars into insignificance, and I have a refutation of Ursus to write. If you will excuse me...

GUNSTADT

But our plan...

KEPLER

I am not interested in your plan. In a week's time...

JEPP

Herr Kepler is right. In a week's time...

GUNSTADT

Yes, in a week's time, then.

KEPLER

A week's time?

GUNSTADT

If you will excuse me, Herr Kepler, I shall go to bed. I have been up half the night and am very tired.

JEPP

As well you should be, Herr Gunstadt. Between servicing Marie, going through Herr Kepler's effects, and trying to steal data from Herr Brahe, I doubt if you caught a wink of sleep.

KEPLER

Going through my effects!

GUNSTADT

(*Embarrassed*) I...

KEPLER

How dare you, sir!

JEPP

You see, Herr Kepler? There is no trust here in Banatky Castle. Not while Herr Brahe is master. Until you learn your way around the secret passageways, until you learn to trust no one...

KEPLER

Secret passageways?

JEPP

Yes, like the secret passage from Herr Brahe's apartment to your room at the end of the corridor. Even now, though I left him sleeping in there (*Nodding toward the room behind him*), who knows but what he isn't in your room at this very moment going through your papers, looking for ideas he can steal.

KEPLER

But I have nothing to hide! He is welcome...

JEPP

If only he could believe you, Herr Kepler. But Herr Brahe, I'm afraid, trusts no one. He thinks you are deceiving him, as he is surely deceiving you.

KEPLER

But he has expressed a willingness to share...

GUNSTADT

If you share your ideas with him in return for his observations, you will find yourself giving much and getting little.

JEPP
Herr Brahe sits over his treasure like a toothless dog over a bone.

GUNSTADT
You might best listen to our plan, Herr Kepler.

KEPLER
In all good conscience, I cannot, gentlemen, if you mean...

JEPP
We mean to make you a present of Herr Brahe's observations, Herr Kepler,
and of you and them to a nobleman worthy of seeing them published to the
world.

GUNSTADT
We mean to be the benefactors of mankind, sir.

KEPLER
I think you mean to be thieves, gentlemen. (*Rising*) I will not be a party to
such skullduggery!

JEPP
(*Frightened*) If we have offended you, Herr Kepler, I am truly sorry.

GUNSTADT
I, too, offer my apologies, Herr Kepler.

JEPP
I trust you will not mention to Herr Brahe what we have shared in confidence?

KEPLER
What kind of scoundrel do you take me for!

JEPP
No scoundrel, sir.

KEPLER
Then let us not speak of it again. Good day, gentlemen.

JEPP
Good day, sir.

GUNSTADT

Good night, Herr Kepler.

KEPLER

(*Starts to exit, then stops, turns, and looks thoughtfully at Jepp*) You say you know where Tycho keeps his observations?

JEPP

Yes, Herr Kepler.

KEPLER

All of them?

JEPP

Yes.

KEPLER

From the very first sighting thirty-five years ago to the last?

JEPP

Yes, Herr Kepler. He keeps them in several large folio volumes hidden...

KEPLER

Several?

JEPP

Yes. Chock-a-block with columns of figures in a small hand. Which, of course, I cannot read, not being literate. But, then, few men can. Only scoundrels and scholars...

KEPLER

Yes, yes...well...I have work to do. Good day, gentlemen.

JEPP and GUNSTADT (*Together*)

(*Jump up as Kepler exits and, clasping hands, dance in a circle, shouting*) He's ours, he's ours! We're rich, we're rich! Revenge! Revenge! (*The door to Tycho's apartment opens and* TYCHO, *half asleep, stumbles into the room*)

TYCHO

(*Roaring*) What the hell is going on here? (*Blackout*)

(*End of Scene Five*)
END OF ACT ONE

ACT TWO

Scene One

At Rise: *Scene same as in Act I. It is two months later, midday April 5, 1600. The sky seen through the high windows appears lighter, the characters wear lighter clothing, and the sound of birds confirms it is spring.* KEPLER, *at the desk, is writing. After some moments, he dips his pen in the ink.*

KEPLER

(*Hesitating*) Furthermore...furthermore...drat! (*Throws the pen down*) I can't concentrate. The bastard won't even let me sleep in the daytime now! (*Unaware of JEPP, who slips into the room through the large door behind him*) How am I to go on? This odorous task will be the death of me. My health...

JEPP

What odious task, Herr Kepler?

KEPLER

(*Startled*) Oh, it's you! Must you skulk around?

JEPP

Skulking is what the master would have me do, Herr Kepler.

KEPLER

Varlet!

JEPP

Yes, yes, and a knave. I am my master's eyes and ears. What odious task, Herr Kepler?

KEPLER

(*Waving sheets of paper at him*) This...this...In Defense of Tycho against Ursus. It will not reflect well on either of us.

JEPP

It seems to me you reflect very well the glory of my master, sir, playing the moon to his sun.

KEPLER
It is a role I do not play well. Does the "great man" still sleep?

JEPP
He will rise soon, sir. It was but a moment ago that I went through his room
and he stirred, growling at me in his sleep.

KEPLER
Then I best put this paper away.

JEPP
But the master will be pleased to find you working on it. I heard him complain
only yesterday, to Joergen, that he is displeased with your progress on the
report you are writing in his defense.

KEPLER
No, no, this is not the report In Defense of Tycho against Ursus. It is...some
...some...private matter.

JEPP
Private matter?

KEPLER
Yes. It does not concern you.

JEPP
But I am most assuredly concerned, sir, with what you write. When the master
is upset, I am apt to suffer more than most, being closer to hand than most.
And while he did not expect you to solve the orbit of Mars in eight days, nor
in the eight weeks that have passed since your arrival, he did expect you to
have at least made a considerable start on his defense against Ursus.

KEPLER
This...this... (*Holding up a sheet of paper*) is nothing. It is but a draft...not
meant for anyone's eyes.

JEPP
A draft, Herr Kepler? Of what?

KEPLER
Of the conditions...but this is a private matter.

JEPP

What conditions, sir?

KEPLER

(*Scowling*) Of the conditions which must prevail if I am to continue this...this "collaboration" with Herr Brahe.

JEPP

Surely you wouldn't quit us!

KEPLER

Not if my conditions are met.

JEPP

If not, you would leave Benatky?!

KEPLER

I have no choice. He treats me like an inferior!

JEPP

That is just his way, Herr Kepler. He treats everyone as an inferior, even the Emperor. Clearly, you are his superior in your ability to make sense of the stars. It is apparent to us all.

KEPLER

(*Angrily*) He seats me at the foot of the table.

JEPP

But sir...

KEPLER

If I and my family are to stay, it is essential I have my own apartment. I cannot put up any longer with the noise and disorder of his household. They distract me...and affect my gall.

JEPP

I have noticed lately a greater number of choleric outbursts than usual, Herr Kepler.

KEPLER

I must be supplied with adequate quantities of firewood, meat, fish, beer, bread, and wine.

JEPP

But sir...

KEPLER

And Herr Brahe must obtain a salary for me from the Emperor.

JEPP

(*Astounded*) A salary!

KEPLER

And in the meantime pay me fifty florins a quarter.

JEPP

(*Aside*) Now he is really going too far!

KEPLER

Most important of all, he must leave me free to choose the time and subject of my research, and to undertake only such tasks as are directly connected with it.

MARIE

(*Rushes in from the corridor, out of breath*) Oh, sir...

JEPP

(*At the same time*) But, sir...

KEPLER

(*Swivels his head from one to the other*) Yes? Yes?

JEPP and MARIE (*Together*)

Sir...

JEPP

(*To Marie*) Age before beauty.

MARIE

(*Confounded*) I...

KEPLER

Calmly. Say what you were going to say.

MARIE

Oh, sir, sir, a professor Jessenius is at the gate. At least he says he is a professor...I cannot tell...of medicine, from Wittenberg. But the master still sleeps. Shall I let him in, sir?

KEPLER

Yes, you may bring him up here. No, wait, Herr Brahe may not like that. He will be afraid for his data. Where is he, Marie? I will go to him...

MARIE

He is in the front hall now, sir. I did not have the heart to keep him waiting outside. He seemed afraid of the dogs.

KEPLER

(*To Jepp*) I will be back in a moment.

JEPP

(*Making a mock bow*) I await your return, Herr Kepler.

MARIE

Follow me, sir. (*Exits with KEPLER following*)

JEPP

(*Runs to the desk after they exit, grabs the sheet of paper Kepler has left there, and waves it aloft*) Now, Herr Kepler, we shall see what we shall see. I have not eyes for such a matter as this, but Tycho has. And he shall reward me well! (*Exits front right, to Tycho's apartment, leaving the stage empty*)

MARIE

(*Enters after a moment or two and looks around*) Where is that Jepp? Every time he is needed he can't be found. Herr Jessenius must have his bags brought in. It seems he is to stay. Herr Kepler has shown him into one of the guest rooms.

KEPLER

(*Enters, bumping into MARIE as she is about to exit*) I...I'm...so sorry. I was worried about...where is Jepp?

MARIE

I'm sure I don't know, sir. I'm looking for him myself. He wasn't here when I came in.

KEPLER

Not here!?

MARIE

No, sir. (*Exits*)

KEPLER

(*Rushes to the desk and searches frantically for his manuscript*) It's not here! It's not here! (*Shouting*) Marie! (*Silence*) Marie!

MARIE

(*Rushes in from the corridor*) Oh, sir! What has happened?

KEPLER

(*Agitated*) My draft, my draft, have you seen my draft?

MARIE

(*Curtsying*) Begging your pardon, sir, but I wouldn't know a draft if I saw one. Have you looked under the table?

KEPLER

The table? Yes. Of course! Jepp! (*Rushes to the table and parts the cloth*) Nothing. I should have known. The traitor!

TYCHO

(*Enters from his apartment, waves the missing sheet of paper in the air, and roars*) What is the meaning of this!

MARIE

Oh, sir, Herr Kepler has lost his draft, but I don't know what it looks like.

TYCHO

(*Roaring*) Out, out! Out of here, wench! Herr Kepler and I have a bone to pick. (*Waves the paper at Kepler after MARIE exits*) So this...this detestable...rot...is what you waste your time on instead of working on the tasks I assign you! No wonder, after eight long weeks, you have no clearer idea of the orbit of Mars than before. And where is my defense against Ursus? Have you forgotten that, too, Herr Kepler?

KEPLER

That...that document...was not meant for your perusal, Herr Brahe.

TYCHO

Not meant for my perusal? It's addressed to me!

KEPLER

It is only a draft. I meant to discuss it with someone...who could give me an objective opinion before...

TYCHO

Discuss it with a member of my staff?

KEPLER

No, no...someone who could be objective. Professor Jessenius...

TYCHO

Jessenius! Is he here? Now?

KEPLER

Yes, he has agreed...

TYCHO

Why wasn't I informed?

KEPLER

You were asleep, sir, and I, Marie, didn't want to wake you. She asked me...I showed him into one of the guest rooms downstairs.

TYCHO

Jessenius here already! And you have met him, sir?

KEPLER

Yes, I...

TYCHO

(*Softening*) You are my prized assistant. (*Puts his arm around Kepler's shoulders*) I invited him here especially to meet you...the famed Kepler, so...so that I might show you off, as it were.

KEPLER

That is hardly modest, sir.

TYCHO

There is no need for modesty at this juncture, Herr Kepler. I have approached the Emperor concerning your employment, and if Jessenius carries a favorable opinion of you back to Prague...

KEPLER

You have spoken to the Emperor about employing me!? Here? For money?

TYCHO

(*Genially*) Yes, yes...come. (*Walking Kepler toward the door*) Let me give you a proper introduction to Jessenius.

KEPLER

He seemed most sympathetic...

TYCHO

You did right to seek his advice.

KEPLER

Objective opinion.

TYCHO

You let trivia upset you.

KEPLER

Trivia!?

TYCHO

You attack with the vehemence of a mad dog when you feel put upon, Herr Kepler, but I assure you, these points can be negotiated in a civilized manner.

KEPLER

I am willing to try.

TYCHO

Then let us discuss them over the dinner table, as two gentlemen, two collaborators, working on the same great project, seeking the same great goal. Herr Jessenius shall be our witness. What say you?

KEPLER

An outside opinion might be helpful.

TYCHO

Good. You give me a voracious appetite, sir. (*THEY exit*)

(*End of Scene One*)

Scene Two

At Rise: *Scene same as before, two hours later. We hear*
              TYCHO and KEPLER quarreling loudly in the hall.
              KEPLER enters, then turns back toward the door.

KEPLER

(*Shouts angrily*) I will decide how best to use my time. Not you! (*Turns to the audience*) The arrogant bastard!

TYCHO

(*Entering, his face flushed*) How dare you, sir, abuse my hospitality! I am the master here and must run this observatory for the greater good of all. I will not have...

KEPLER

You dig your spurs into me as if I were a flagging beast of burden. I am in need, not of a spur, but rather of a brake to prevent the threat of galloping consumption due to overwork.

TYCHO

Your constant mewling, whining, and self-pity disgusts me. I ask nothing of you that I do not ask of myself.

KEPLER

You sleep till noon, sir, while I, who work deep into the night, am not allowed to rest in the daytime, but must work on this odious refutation of the Bear's scurrilous attacks, though the man is dead and no one...

TYCHO

I will not keep anyone on the staff who cannot, with goodwill, undertake the tasks assigned to him.

KEPLER

And I will not continue to work with someone who so disrespects my needs as a human being and as a...a...natural philosopher.

TYCHO

I have acceded to your every wish--the private apartment for you and your family, the provisions, including wine, to be supplied by me. And I have applied to the Emperor for your employment. But I will not take direction from you on how to run my laboratory!

KEPLER

And I, sir, will not take direction from you on how and when to do my research! I am not your apprentice, I am your equal!

TYCHO

(*Roaring*) You forget, sir, who is imperial mathematicus...and who heads this laboratory!

KEPLER

How could I forget? You make that impossible!

TYCHO

You are insolent, sir! I will not put up with...

KEPLER

After tomorrow that won't be necessary.

TYCHO

Even Jessenius agreed that a laboratory cannot have two heads. Either you obey my orders or...(*Startled*) What are you saying?

KEPLER

I have made arrangements to leave for Prague...

TYCHO

Leave for Prague! But what...who...

KEPLER

With Herr Jessenius. Baron Hoffman has offered me quarters.

TYCHO

Fool!

KEPLER

I shall convey your message to him.

TYCHO

It is not Baron Hoffman who is the fool, but yourself, sir. You said yourself that here is where your destiny lies.

KEPLER

I must have misread my horoscope.

TYCHO

You need my observations to prove your theories.

KEPLER

What observations? You do not let me see them. In two month's time you have disgorged but a few, and those only out of necessity, since they relate to Mars. The rest remain inaccessible.

TYCHO

The remaining observations will be forthcoming when...

KEPLER

I no longer believe in your promises, Herr Brahe.

TYCHO

You dare to question my integrity?

KEPLER

I had also to badger you about the compensation you promised me.

TYCHO

It has been but a week or two since I applied to the Emperor...

KEPLER

For lack of funds, my family lingers in Graz, waiting to join me. It is clear I must make other arrangements.

TYCHO

Be patient but a few days longer, I beseech you. Until we hear from the Emperor.

KEPLER

It will make no difference. My mind is made up. I can no longer tolerate your tyrannical ways...

TYCHO

Tyrannical ways! I am the very soul of kindness.

KEPLER

And your lack of trust.

TYCHO

Lack of trust!

KEPLER

There is no future for me here...

TYCHO

If anything, I am too trusting...a very paragon of virtue in that regard, sir. How dare you accuse me...

KEPLER

Not only do you not trust me with your observations, but you took notes of our discussion before Jessenius at the supper table and made him be witness to them! That was the last straw.

TYCHO

That was but good business practice.

KEPLER

I did not come here to work with a...a...merchant...but with Tycho Brahe the astronomer.

TYCHO

My head may be in the stars, Herr Kepler, but, unlike you, my feet are on the ground.

KEPLER

You have the soul of a merchant, sir.

TYCHO

And you, sir, are insulting. I must ask you to keep a civil tongue in your head, or...or choose your weapon. You will not be the first man I have fought in a duel.

KEPLER

That is as plain as the nose on your face.

TYCHO

(*Slaps Kepler and roars*) Choose your weapon!

KEPLER

(*Backing away, hand on cheek*) T-T-Truth is my weapon.

TYCHO
The truth is in my observations, which you will never see!

KEPLER
It is as I thought. There is no point in my staying.

TYCHO
Go, then! Who is begging you to stay?

KEPLER
I go...tomorrow.

TYCHO
Good riddance to bad rubbish!

KEPLER
You dare say that to me?

TYCHO
I say what it pleases me to say.

KEPLER
You are rude, sir...a petty despot...a swaggering bully...a braggart...a pompous ass...a...

TYCHO
(*Beside himself with rage*) Out! Out! Out of my sight!

KEPLER
Even the stars could not make me stay. (*To audience*) Have you ever seen such a son of a bitch? (*Storms out*)

TYCHO
(*Waving his fist after him*) Thief! Parasite! Ingrate! (*Gradually his anger abates*) You will be back! You need me. Your theories... (*Flatly*) are nothing without...my observations. (*Looks at audience*) Am I mad? (*Anguished*) It is I who need him! My observations are nothing without his genius to make sense of them. (*Calls*) Herr Kepler! (*Louder*) Herr Kepler! (*Starts toward door, then stops and returns thoughtfully to stage front, where he strikes an arrogant pose. To audience*) Let him go! He will come crawling back to me like the worm he is. You shall see.

(*End of Scene Two*)

Scene Three

At Rise: *Same scene, a week later. TYCHO and GUNSTADT are*
                    seated at the supper table. TYCHO reads a letter
                    while GUNSTADT, picking his teeth and sipping wine,
                    listens. JEPP, beneath the table, gnaws on a bone.

TYCHO

Listen to what Herr Kepler writes. "The criminal hand which, the other day, was quicker than the wind in inflicting injury hardly knows how to set about it to make amends." What did I tell you?

JEPP

Yes, yes...what did he tell us?

TYCHO

Didn't I tell you he would come crawling back?

JEPP

Yes, yes...you told us he would come crawling back, like a worm. (*Holding his bone to the floor*) Here wormy, wormy. Here worm.

TYCHO

He blames the quarrel on his lack of self-control.

GUNSTADT

He has an unnatural temper, sir. You were right to send him away.

JEPP

Strange people, these geniuses. One is more than enough.

TYCHO

But he apologizes. Listen. "For two months you most generously provided for my needs...you extended me every friendship...you allowed me to share in your most treasured possessions..."

JEPP

(*Astonished*) He, too, shared Marie?!

TYCHO

(*Reading*) "Neither to your children, nor to your wife, nor to yourself did you devote yourself more than to me..." That's the God's truth! A pain in the ass if ever there was one.

JEPP

Herr Gunstadt will kiss the boo-boo.

GUNSTADT

You are a patient man, Herr Brahe.

TYCHO

He speaks of his "sick mind."

GUNSTADT

'Tis fitting that he should recognize it. At least he is honest.

JEPP

He is a worm.

TYCHO

He knows his faults.

JEPP

Which is more than most.

TYCHO

Listen to what he writes. "Instead of displaying moderation, I indulged during three weeks with closed eyes in sullen stubbornness against you and your family..."

JEPP

A most persistent man...a sign of genius.

TYCHO

"Instead of thanking you, I displayed blind rage..."

JEPP

A most passionate man!

TYCHO

"Instead of showing you respect, I displayed the greatest insolence against your person, which by noble descent, prominent learning, and great fame deserves all respect..."

                              JEPP
The ungrateful cur!

                              TYCHO
"Instead of sending you a friendly greeting, I let myself be carried away by
suspicion and insinuation when I was itching with bitterness..."

                              JEPP
(*Scratching himself*) Scratch, scratch.

                              TYCHO
"I never considered how cruelly I must have hurt you by this despicable
behavior."

                              JEPP
Poor Tycho!

                              TYCHO
(*Wiping away a tear*) I am moved.

                              JEPP
The sun is moved by Kepler's force.

                              TYCHO
I have misjudged him, Herr Gunstadt. The man is most contrite...

                            GUNSTADT
You are too kind, sir.

                              TYCHO
It is one of my failings.

                              JEPP
One of many.

                              MARIE
(*Enters excitedly*) Sir! Sir! Herr Kepler...

                              TYCHO
Herr Kepler?

                              MARIE
Is here!

TYCHO

In the castle?

MARIE

Yes, sire.

TYCHO

I gave strict orders...

MARIE

I could not keep him out.

TYCHO

The scoundrel!

JEPP

Now we shall see if the moon can eclipse the sun.

KEPLER

(*Enters, excited*) Herr Brahe! (*Falls to his knees*) I come to you as a postulant to ask, in the name of divine pity, for your forgiveness of my terrible offenses.

TYCHO

(*Too astonished to speak*) I...uh...

KEPLER

What I have said or written against your person, your fame, your honor, your scientific rank...I now retract and declare, voluntarily and freely, invalid, false, and unsound...

JEPP

The man has a way with words.

TYCHO

Please, Herr Kepler. There is no need...

KEPLER

And I promise henceforth to refrain from such foolish acts and words...

JEPP

A most foolish vow.

TYCHO
Enough, Herr Kepler. Rise. Consider the matter forgotten.

KEPLER
I shall never again, in any way, unjustly and deliberately offend you again, sir.

TYCHO
(*Trying to be patient*) Rise, Herr Kepler. There is no need for such an abject apology. It was but a misunderstanding.

KEPLER
(*As TYCHO helps him to his feet*) You are too kind, sir.

GUNSTADT
(*Aside*) Just what I was saying!

TYCHO
Not at all. (*Puts his arm about Kepler's shoulders*) We are the closest of friends. (*Falsely genial*) We welcome you back with open arms and...and...an open...heart.

JEPP
But not with open books.

KEPLER
You are most magnanimous.

TYCHO
It is nothing.

JEPP
My master speaks the truth.

TYCHO
The work we do is too important to let trivia come between us. We are rational men...astronomers...

JEPP
Fools.

KEPLER
Collaborators.

TYCHO

(*Reluctantly*) Ye-e-s...even that.

KEPLER

Then we are friends?

TYCHO

Most assuredly.

KEPLER

If you notice any tendency in me in the future toward such unwise manner of behavior, Herr Brahe, I would have you point it out.

TYCHO

I am sure there will be no need.

KEPLER

You will find me willing to change.

TYCHO

(*Impatiently*) Yes, yes.

KEPLER

I promise to oblige you by all kinds of services, and by my acts prove to you that my attitude toward you has changed.

TYCHO

What's passed is past.

KEPLER

I pray that God may help me to fulfill this promise.

TYCHO

(*Exploding*) Enough, Herr Kepler! (*Angrily, to the others who have been watching this performance*) What are you gaping at, jackanapes! Have you nothing better to do? (*To Marie*). Bring more food, and beer and wine. Herr Kepler...

KEPLER

No beer or wine, sir. Spirituous liquors...

TYCHO

(*To Gunstadt*) Go! See that Herr Kepler's new quarters are made ready.

KEPLER

New quarters!

TYCHO

I have given you your own apartment, as you requested, so that you and your family...

KEPLER

My family! Your goodness overwhelms me, sir. I will be forever in your debt...

JEPP

(*Mocking*) Your goodness overwhelms...

TYCHO

(*To Jepp, ominously*) You go too far...

JEPP

(*Bowing obsequiously*) Yes, master. (*Turns his behind on Tycho*) I will be forever in your debt.

TYCHO

Out, out, little monster! (*Gives Jepp a boot that sends him flying toward the door. To Kepler, as if in apology*) I am surrounded by imbeciles!

JEPP

But at Benatky there is always room for one more.

TYCHO

(*Roaring*) Go! (*JEPP makes an obscene gesture. TYCHO grabs a plate from the table and throws it at him. JEPP exits as the plate smashes against the door or on the floor. BLACK OUT*)

(*End of Scene Three*)

Scene Four

At Rise: *Same scene, year and a half later, October 24, 1601, evening.* KEPLER *and* GUNSTADT *stand on darkened stage, backs to the audience. Sound of weeping can be heard.* MARIE *enters through door at stage left carrying a lantern. Sets it on table and starts to exit, but stops when she hears the weeping. Glances at Kepler and Gunstadt, then crosses to table and pulls back cloth to reveal weeping Jepp.*

MARIE
Now, now, little man, you take it too hard.

JEPP
I cannot help it.

MARIE
He was a monster.

JEPP
But...but...I loved him! (*As he speak, ghost of* TYCHO *enters from his apartment and stands quietly, head bowed, hands clasped in front of him*)

MARIE
His death was in keeping with the way he lived.

TYCHO
It is but a scant eleven days since I was taken ill.

KEPLER
(*Turning, with* GUNSTADT, *to face the audience, to whom he speaks in a solemn tone*) On October 13, 1601, Tycho Brahe, in the company of Master Minkowitz, had dinner at the illustrious Baron Rosenberg's table in Prague.

GUNSTADT
It must have been an illustrious company. There was even an imperial councilor among the guests.

MARIE
Herr Brahe was used to illustrious company. He entertained royalty here at

Benatky. It was my privilege to wait on them.

GUNSTADT
It's difficult to understand why he couldn't handle the predicament in which he found himself.

JEPP
(*To audience*) He had to pee.

GUNSTADT
He was accustomed to vast amounts of drink. It shouldn't have been a problem.

KEPLER
He held back his water beyond the demands of courtesy. When he drank more, he felt the tension in his bladder increase, but he put politeness before his health.

GUNSTADT
When he got home, he was scarcely able to urinate.

TYCHO
(*Crosses to the cot and lies down. Tosses and turns, groaning*) Oh, oh, oh...

KEPLER
After five sleepless nights, he could still only pass his water with the greatest pain, and even so, the passage was impeded.

MARIE
There was nothing I could do for him.

JEPP
It was impossible to amuse him.

KEPLER
The insomnia continued, with internal fever gradually leading to delirium.

TYCHO
(*Shouting*) You bloody little beast! By God, I'll have you drawn and quartered!

JEPP
Even at the last, I was the one most on his mind.

TYCHO

(*Shouting*) Where is my food, bitch? Are you trying to starve me to death?!

MARIE

And I.

KEPLER

The food he ate, from which he could not be kept, exacerbated the evil.

MARIE

He ate ravenously whatever dish he ordered.

JEPP

He died a glutton's death.

KEPLER

On his last night, in his gentle delirium, he kept repeating...

TYCHO

Ne frusta vixisse videar...ne frusta vixisse videar...

GUNSTADT

Let me not seem to have lived in vain.

KEPLER

He repeated the words over and over, like someone composing a poem.

TYCHO

Ne frusta vixisse videar...ne frusta vixisse videar...

GUNSTADT

Let me not seem to have lived in vain.

KEPLER

No doubt he wished that these words should be added to the title page of his works, thus dedicating them to the memory and uses of posterity.

JEPP

No doubt he was afraid his life would seem wasted to posterity unless someone built a monument to him based on his observations.

GUNSTADT

He wanted Kepler to build that monument, the new universe, on the Tychonic, not the Copernican, system.

KEPLER

It was his last wish.

JEPP

He never stopped trying to impose his own idea of the universe on Herr Kepler.

MARIE

Poor Tycho.

JEPP

He should have known. Now Herr Kepler will do just the opposite. He will use Herr Brahe's data to prove the system of Copernicus.

MARIE

I shall miss him.

GUNSTADT

His family must be notified.

JEPP

The observations must not be allowed to fall into their hands.

KEPLER

(*Suddenly aware of the situation*) Get them...hide them...in my quarters...beneath the stones.

MARIE

The Junker Tengnagel will be furious.

KEPLER

It doesn't matter. It was Herr Brahe's last wish...that I should build the new universe.

JEPP/MARIE/GUNSTADT (*Together*)

Yes.

KEPLER

(*Speaking as if reading an announcement, HE and the OTHERS slowly gather about the cot on which Tycho lies peaceful and still*) On October 24, Tycho Brahe's delirium ceased for several hours...nature conquered...and he expired peacefully among the consolations, prayers, and tears of his people. (*Slow fade-out as* KEPLER *and the* OTHERS *lament in silent mimicry, until the stage is dark. Then a spotlight shines on the stage front center. While the others remain frozen in their lamentations in the shadows,* GUNSTADT *steps into the spot*)

GUNSTADT

(*To audience*) Tycho de Brahe, to give him his full and lordly name, was buried in Prague on November 4, 1601, amidst much pomp and splendor. Twelve imperial gentlemen-at-arms, following after his coat of arms, his golden spurs, and his favorite horse, carried his coffin to the grave. Two days later, on November 6th, the Emperor's privy councilor, Herr Barwitz, called on Kepler here at Benatky to announce that Kepler had been appointed to succeed Tycho as imperial mathematicus. (*Lights up*)

ALL

(*Loudly, jumping up and throwing their arms in the air*) Hurrah!

KEPLER

The observations!

MARIE

We must find them!

GUNSTADT

We must hide them!

JEPP

Follow me!

(*There is a made scramble for the door to Tycho's apartment stage right. Black out*)

(*End of Scene Four*)

Scene Five

At Rise: *Same scene, eleven years later, January 20, 1612.*
JEPP and MARIE, stage rear, are attempting to cover
the quadrant with a sheet. Accomplishing this, THEY
gather some of the smaller instruments together and
put them in gunny sacks. Meanwhile KEPLER, deeply
depressed, sits at the desk, his back to the audience.

JEPP

I don't see why we have to move just because the Emperor died.

MARIE

Herr Kepler has lost his job. The new emperor, whoever he may be, will want
to appoint his own imperial mathematicus.

JEPP

But why can't we stay on here at Benatky?

MARIE

The castle goes with the job.

JEPP

Balls!

MARIE

Don't be vulgar. If the master hears you...

TYCHO

(*Enters as Jepp and Marie quarrel and stands quietly to one side of the door,*
rear, his hands folded before him as before. Only Kepler can hear and see
him) So, Rudolph has died?

KEPLER

Yes.

TYCHO

Such a pity.

KEPLER

He had a weak temperament. They say he was mad at the end and was kept a prisoner in his own citadel. His cousin Leopold...

TYCHO

At least he provided for you?

KEPLER

If promises are provisions, yes. But one had to be the devil's own disciple to get any actual monies from him.

MARIE

(*Distressed by Kepler's speech to the empty air*) Master? You spoke?

KEPLER

(*Startled*) No...it is nothing. I was but speaking to myself. (*JEPP whirls his finger about his temple to indicate he thinks Kepler has gone mad. With MARIE, continues packing*)

TYCHO

I win the bet. It took you not eight days, but eight years, to determine the orbit of Mars.

KEPLER

Five years. It took another four years to get my manuscript published. Not only was there no money to pay the printer, but Junker Tengnagel made things difficult.

TYCHO

That asshole!

KEPLER

He had his reasons. I must confess that when you died, I quickly took advantage of the absence, or lack of circumspection, of your heirs, by taking the observations under my care...

TYCHO

You dog. You stole them!

KEPLER

Well...yes, you might say I "usurped" them.

TYCHO

That's what I do say.

KEPLER

I apologize.

TYCHO

No need. That's what I wanted you to do. You were the only one…but, damn you, you used them to prove Copernicus right!

KEPLER

It couldn't be helped.

TYCHO

I suppose not. And Tengnagel?

KEPLER

He grabbed what he could, mostly your instruments, and kept them under lock and key, where they rusted to scrap metal. The same fate might have befallen your observations if I hadn't "stolen" them. It was for the sake of posterity.

TYCHO

The junker is an idiot! What did he want? Money?

KEPLER

Fame. He wanted his name as co-author on my manuscript, and on all future works.

TYCHO

The dastard! Daughter or no, I would have skewered him.

KEPLER

I was more concerned that the Truth be promulgated…

TYCHO

What are you saying?

KEPLER

That I acceded to his demand.

TYCHO

You agreed!

KEPLER

Providing he hand over in exchange one-quarter of the thousand thalers he was then receiving as your son-in-law each year from the treasury. But he balked.

The deal fell through.

TYCHO

The fool! He held immortality in his hand....Is that why you let him write the preface?

KEPLER

Yes. It was the only way I could get his permission to publish.

TYCHO

But you had the observations in your possession. Though, technically, he was my heir, you could have...

KEPLER

A few years ago he embraced the Catholic faith and was made an appellate councilor at court, which enabled him to impose his conditions on me.

TYCHO

The mediocre are the bane of anyone with talent or intelligence. I never liked him. What did you do?

KEPLER

What could I do? I was tied hand and foot. Tengnagel sat on your treasure like a dog in the manger, unable to put the data to use himself, but nevertheless preventing others from doing so.

TYCHO

So you let him meddle in your work?

KEPLER

Permitting him to write the preface was the only acceptable compromise.

TYCHO

His preface reads like the braying of an ass.

KEPLER

No matter. No one will remember him.

TYCHO

I like your title.

A NEW ASTRONOMY Based on Causation
or A PHYSICS OF THE SKY
derived from Investigations of the

MOTIONS OF THE STAR MARS
Founded on Observations of
THE NOBLE TYCHO BRAHE

You proved me wrong, but at least you gave me my due.

MARIE

(*In a loud whisper to Jepp*) Perhaps we should get help...

JEPP

Maybe Herr Gunstadt...

MARIE

(*To Kepler*) Herr Kepler? Sir? We need more gunny sacks and string for the packing...

KEPLER

(*To Tycho*) I couldn't in good conscience have done otherwise.

MARIE

(*Frightened now*) Sir? Jepp and I...

KEPLER

(*Suddenly aware of her. Impatiently*) Go, go!

TYCHO

(*As JEPP and MARIE scamper out*) They think you mad.

KEPLER

What does it matter? Half the world thinks me mad. Even Maestlin does not write, though I sent him a copy of the New Astronomy, knowing he shares my views. Even the most enlightened...

TYCHO

It will take time.

KEPLER

(*Searches among the papers on his desk and comes up with a letter*) Here, this is from Johann Brengger, a most liberal scholar, a man in tune with our modern views.

TYCHO

Yes, yes, I am aware of him.

KEPLER

He writes, in response to a letter of my own: "When you say that you aim at teaching both a new physics of the sky and a new kind of mathematics, based not on circles but on magnetic and intelligent forces, I rejoice with you, although I must frankly confess that I am unable to imagine, and even less to comprehend, such a mathematical procedure."

TYCHO

You are ahead of your time, Herr Kepler. We both were. You stand at the threshold of a new age...an age of science...of mathematical truths. Your Laws of planetary motion will make you immortal. On them will be built...

KEPLER

Pah! They are nothing...dung I dragged in to clear out greater dung... mathematical "tricks" to help us better understand the harmony of the spheres.

TYCHO

They are the foundation stones on which Newton will build his theory of universal gravitation.

KEPLER

Gravitation?

TYCHO

The force you hinted at in your introduction. The force that keeps the planets circling the sun and the moon circling the earth. You see, I admit you were right, Herr Kepler.

KEPLER

You are too kind.

TYCHO

No, no. You pointed the way. You said there must be a force, the anima motrix you called it, emanating from the sun, that drives the planets round in their orbits. Newton took his cue from you.

KEPLER

I do not know the name.

TYCHO

Sixty years from now he will build the modern universe on the basis of your planetary laws, a universe that turns forever with clockwork regularity. It is the universe you described.

KEPLER

The mathematical harmony of the world.

TYCHO

Yes. It is what cosmologists will still be seeking five hundred years from now, a single equation that will explain the All.

KEPLER

God.

TYCHO

Yes. Newton may build the modern universe, but he will confess that if he has seen further than most men, it is because he has stood on the shoulders of giants. You are one of those giants, Herr Kepler.

KEPLER

But without your observations...

TYCHO

Yes, yes...I have my place in history, but you...

KEPLER

I? I have taken a giant step backwards. I have been offered the position of mathematicus at Linz and have decided to accept it. Forty-one years old, and I am back where I was at twenty-three, teaching nincompoops and casting horoscopes to make a living in a provincial town in Upper Austria.

TYCHO

No matter. You have great work yet to do. Your Third Law...

KEPLER

Perhaps it is just as well. The war that has broken out makes it difficult to work here. To better defend themselves, the soldiers have deforested the woods about Prague, and already there has been bloody fighting in the town. In Linz, at least, I will be free from the worst of the horrors. The war can't go on forever.

TYCHO

It will go on for thirty years. But these are matters of the moment. Your work...

KEPLER

Did I tell you Barbara died? And my son Frederich? The portents should have warned me. Besides the war, the year 1611 brought epidemics to Prague, and Barbara, being in frail health...

TYCHO

I didn't know...about your wife, I mean.

KEPLER

First she contracted the Hungarian fever, then, when it seemed she was getting better, the children came down with pox, which the soldiery imported. The oldest and youngest recovered, but poor Frederich...how I grieve for him. He was only six years old...and my favorite child.

TYCHO

Such matters seem of small import to me now, but I have not been so long dead as not to remember what it was like...this human suffering...and I sympathize with you. But fame demands...

KEPLER

What does it signify, this clutching at fame by means of startling projects and unusual actions, the restless search for and interpretation of causes...

TYCHO

It is the search for God in the universe.

KEPLER

The search for the eternal harmonies of the world.

TYCHO

The search for a grand unified theory, relativity, the space-time continuum, quantum mechanics, black holes...

KEPLER

In vain does the God of War growl, snarl, roar, and try to interrupt with bombards, trumpets, and his whole tarantantaran...

TYCHO

Man must seek the Truth.

KEPLER

Let us despise the barbaric neighings which echo through these noble lands, and awaken our understanding and longing for the harmonies.

TYCHO

Having first perceived the first glimmer of dawn...

KEPLER

I give myself up to this holy raving. I mockingly defy all mortals with this open confession.

TYCHO

Nothing shall hold you back.

KEPLER

I have robbed the golden vessels of the Sun to make out of them a tabernacle for my God, far from the frontiers of Heaven.

TYCHO

The universe is One.

KEPLER

(*To God*) If You forgive me, God, I shall rejoice. If You are angry, I shall bear it. Behold, I have cast the dice.

TYCHO

The die is cast!

KEPLER

I shall write a book, either for my contemporaries or for posterity. It is all the same to me. I may wait a hundred years for a reader, since God has waited six thousand years for a witness...

TYCHO

It will wait hardly more than sixty years...for Newton to find buried in its text the three planetary Laws of Motion...

KEPLER

God sets my enthusiasm on fire and stirs in me an irrepressible desire!

TYCHO

The stars wait, Herr Kepler. On, on...to infinity!

KEPLER

(*Shudders. The spell is broken*) The infinite is unthinkable!

TYCHO

(*Deflated*) Immanuel Kant, one of our greatest philosophers, will one day call you the most acute thinker ever born.

KEPLER

I do not know the man.

TYCHO

(*Uncomfortable*) Yes...well...I must go. It is getting late.

KEPLER

But we were just beginning to speak of matters of importance. I have not been well. After Barbara died...I was struck by an insidious fever. On May 31 I took a light laxative, according to habit, and on June 1 I bled myself, also according to habit. No urgent disease, not even the suspicion of one, compelled me to do it, nor any astrological consideration...

TYCHO

Yes, yes...I must be going now. Why don't you try to sleep?

KEPLER

I think I am one of those people whose gall bladder has a direct opening into the stomach. Such people are short-lived as a rule. I always feel the pain, just under my ribs, here...and here...

TYCHO

Yes...well...I must go. Jepp and Marie will be returning with Gunstadt any moment. I left him asleep, but they will find him.

KEPLER

Why don't you stay? They will be happy to see you.

TYCHO

They cannot see me. Only you...our minds...

KEPLER

Yes, yes...such heated discussions we used to have. Should reality be sought on the physical or metaphysical level? How can the earth, or its nature, notice, recognize, and seek after the center of the world, which is only a little point? If the orbit of Mars is egg-shaped, how...

                                TYCHO
There is no time...

                                KEPLER
I miss you. (*Saddened*) I grow old.

                                TYCHO
You will live another twenty years.

                                KEPLER
There is no one left who understands me.

                                TYCHO
You are esteemed everywhere.

                                KEPLER
I get lonelier with each passing year.

                                TYCHO
It doesn't matter. You have work to do.

                                KEPLER
(*Brightening at the mention of work*) I am thinking of publishing my
correspondence with various scholars on the chronology of the life of Christ.
I feel quite certain he was born four or five years B.C., before the date
generally attributed to his birth.

                                TYCHO
Time has proved you right even there, Herr Kepler. But you are getting very
sleepy. Go to sleep now.

                                KEPLER
Yes, yes, I am sleepy. I have not been well lately.

                                TYCHO
Dream of your harmonies, Herr Kepler.

                                KEPLER
(*Alert again*) Actually, there are two kinds of harmonies, Herr Brahe. Those
that reside in sense phenomena, such as the harmonies of music, and then the
pure harmonies, which are constructed of mathematical concepts.

TYCHO
Yes, yes...it grows late, Herr Kepler. Sleep.

KEPLER
(*Yawning*) But soon I will need to wake. The stars... (*Looks up at the night sky through the high windows*) Contrary to what we think, there must be millions of them.

TYCHO
Billions of them, Herr Kepler...in billions of galaxies, an expanding universe curving back in on itself in a space-time continuum...

KEPLER
(*Brightly*) Did you know that Galileo, looking through that new instrument of his, the telescope, found four new planets circling Jupiter?

TYCHO
Moons.

KEPLER
What?

TYCHO
Sleep, Herr Kepler.

KEPLER
(*Yawns*) My day is only beginning. Tell Gunstadt to wake me at twelve...promptly. We must... (*His head drops. TYCHO steps into the shadows, then exits as JEPP, MARIE, and GUNSTADT enter*)

GUNSTADT
(*Stops short when he sees Kepler's inert form*) But Herr Kepler is asleep!

MARIE
Maybe he was talking in his sleep.

JEPP
And dreaming.

GUNSTADT
Or maybe the two of you were. Which is more likely.

KEPLER

(*Stirs, mumbling*) Animus est imago Dei incorporea.

JEPP

The master speaks.

MARIE

What's he saying?

GUNSTADT

Something about God.

JEPP

Bad, bad sleep. Nightmares.

MARIE

Maybe we should wake him.

GUNSTADT

No, no, let him sleep. He will wake soon enough.

JEPP

Look at the silly man. He smiles in his sleep.

MARIE

He is dreaming.

JEPP

But of what?

GUNSTADT

Who knows?

MARIE

Only God knows.

JEPP

And perhaps Herr Kepler.

GUNSTADT

Sh-sh. Don't wake him.